KRAKTO
CHAMPION OF THE WORLD

Other Books by Philip Temple and Chris Gaskin

Moa, the story of a fabulous bird (1985)

The Legend of the Kea (1986)

The Story of the Kakapo, Parrot of the Night (1988)

Kotuku, the flight of the white heron (1994)

The artist wishes to acknowledge the assistance of the Arts Council of New Zealand Toi Aotearoa for this book.

ISBN 1-86958-168-7

Text © 1995 Philip Temple
Illustrations © 1995 Chris Gaskin

Published in 1995 by Hodder Moa Beckett Publishers Limited
[a member of the Hodder Headline Group]
4 Whetu Place, Mairangi Bay, Auckland
PO Box 100-749, North Shore Mail Centre, Auckland 1330

Printed through Colorcraft, Hong Kong

KRAKTO

CHAMPION OF THE WORLD

Story by

Philip Temple

Illustrated by

Chris Gaskin

Hodder Moa Beckett

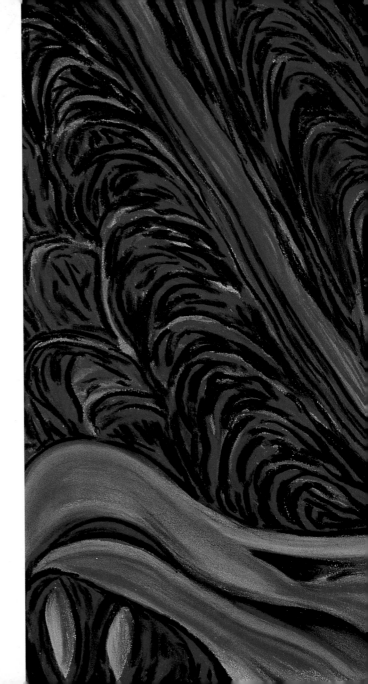

KA, the great bird of all birds, created night, the sun and moon and the stars. His voice sounded like thunder. His eyes flashed like lightning and his feathers reflected the colours of the rainbow. Ka's brother, Antika, created nothing. He had the voice of a dry river. His eyes reflected only darkness and his feathers were the colour of the bottom of the sea.

Ka drove Antika from the nest of the world when they were fledglings. Antika had fouled the nest and tried to steal all the food. He had screamed and screamed against peace and silence. Ka cleaned Antika's poisonous droppings from the forest and shared the world's food among all the birds. He brought peace on all winds.

But Antika remained inside everything because he was forever the brother of Ka. He skulked through the world, hiding in the trunks of trees and feeding through the beaks of other birds. It filled him with a great rage to live only in the form of other things.

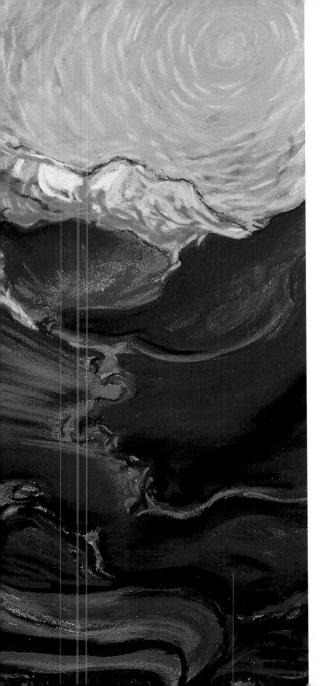

Antika burrowed deep into the earth like a worm until the roots of all trees remained forever twisted. He burrowed beneath the rivers, squeezing them into rapids and fierce currents. He burrowed beneath the sea, upsetting the great waters until they swelled and rolled around the world, trying to escape Antika's endless hate. He burrowed beneath the rocks at the heart of the earth, buckling and bending them into mountains.

Antika's jealousy and rivalry with Ka knew no end. The earth quaked with his rage. The mountains trembled and wept tears of avalanching snow. New hills boiled with Antika's hot pride, exploding with fires that challenged Ka's sun. They scorched Ka's sky, threatening to melt the moon. They made a new night with the clouds of smoke that rose from the burning forests.

Ka brought rain to put out the raging fires and cool winds to calm the storming waters. But these only fanned Antika's anger more. He tried even harder to destroy Ka because now he thought he could bring his own order to the world.

Ka and Antika struggled for eight years. Night and day became one with the fury of their beating wings. The sun became cool, the moon pale and the entire world groaned. The birds clung to the few trees that remained in the forest, eating their own feathers and filling their empty bellies with stones.

The keas Krikta, Starwing and their fledglings – Krakto, Longbeak, Redfeather and Bluetail – had nothing left to eat except ice and their own droppings.

'Hullooo Ka!' Krikta screeched. 'We have had no berries for eight years, the beech trees have moulted and the waters of Star Lake have turned into mist. You started day and night. You decided that flowers and berries would appear only once a year. You gave us all a job and a perch. Now here we are, looking after our own business, doing the right thing, and we have to put up with all this. Rain like there's no end when we're trying to preen our feathers. Endless sun when we're trying to sleep. There's no moon to fly by at night and such a wind that a kea can't put his head out of the nest. I ask you. Is this the best berry on the bush? What kind of deal *is* this, great bird of all birds?'

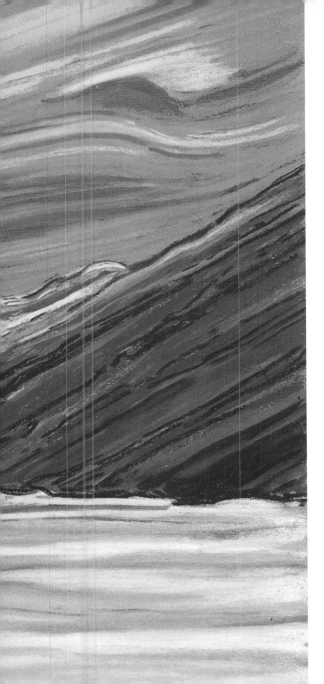

There was a great silence. The sky cleared of rain, the sun shone, the moon rose, the wind dropped and the earth became still. Then the keas saw two gigantic beaks appear and two pairs of eyes glaring at them over the mountains.

'What did you say?' thundered Ka, so that the earth shook again.

Krikta screeched, 'I said it's about time you kept your side of the deal. Are you the great bird of all birds or aren't you?'

Antika cackled with the voice of an avalanche: 'You must be joking. He has the wings of a mosquito, the beak of a tomtit and the bandy legs of a rock wren!'

'And it's taken you eight years to find *that* out?' cried Krikta.

'I am the great bird of all birds!' rumbled Ka. 'Your words are like drops of rain in the desert. The natural order of things will be soon restored. Then all the birds of the world shall live in peace and harmony once more.'

'Just who are you, anyway, shortbeak?' Antika rattled at Krikta.

'*I* am the great bird of all birds. Soon I shall bring a new order to the world, where the berry goes to the biggest beak and sharpest claw. You should do well.'

Krikta said, 'Well, I have an idea that will give us all an easier time.'

'Do you speak for all the birds of the world?' roared Ka.

From the mountains around, from the forests and plains below, from the rivers and lakes and from the great ocean came a chorus of screeches and cackles, screams and shrieks. 'Yay!' cried all the birds in the world.

'What is this idea?' Antika asked suspiciously.

'You each choose a champion, from all the birds that have ever been, to fight for your own order of things.'

All the birds of the world again cried, 'Yay!'

'A fight to the death!' demanded Antika.

'The loser must never again challenge the other,' demanded Ka.

'Choose your champion!' Antika cackled at Ka.

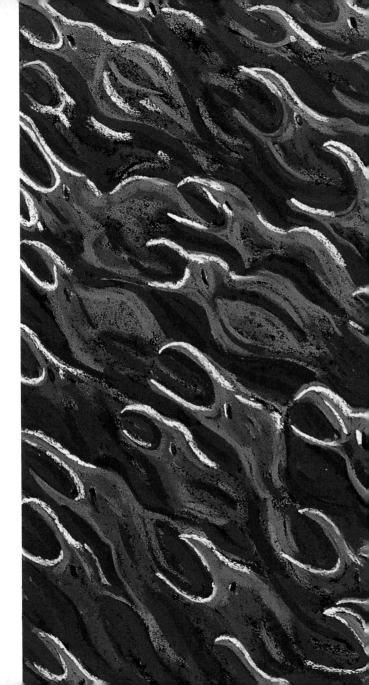

Ka roared, 'I call on the falcon to defend the natural order of things.' But the falcon was nowhere to be found. Then Ka called on the hawk, the morepork and the black-backed gull. He called on all the other birds of the world. No one answered. Suddenly, none were to be found.

Krikta said, 'Looks like me.' Ka closed his eyes and shuddered.

'I'll defend the natural order!' cried Krakto, Krikta's strongest fledgling. 'The time has come to show the power of a kea's wings, the strength of Ka's best beak, the grip of the world's best claws.'

'Easy son,' said Krikta. 'Easy.'

'Against such a champion,' Antika cackled, 'it will be hard to find a challenger.'

'There are no other birds to choose from,' cried Krikta. 'You lose by default.'

'Not so fast, clever-claws,' Antika rumbled. 'A champion can be chosen from all the birds that *ever have been*!'

'Yes. But . . .'

'Then here is my champion!' Antika screamed. He lifted one enormous wing and out flew a great-eagle. Its talons were double the length and sharpness of Krakto's. Its hooked beak could take off his head at one blow. Quietly, Krikta said to Krakto, 'We could try something else, change the rules . . . '

'No!' thundered Antika. 'Let the contest begin. To the death!'

'We need time for a team talk!' Krikta cried.

Ka closed his eyes and shuddered again.

Krikta and Krakto put their heads together. Ka and Antika strained their great ears but could hear nothing of what they said. Antika grew impatient. 'Let the contest begin!' he roared again.

'Keep your feathers on!' cried Krikta. 'Allow me to present . . . Krakto! Champion of the World!' He hopped back to allow his brave fledgling to spread his wings in style.

'And allow me to present,' jeered Antika, 'the Champion of the New World, Moadeath! *Now* can the contest begin?'

'Let the contest begin,' groaned Ka.

The great-eagle swooped on Krakto with all the weight of his great body. His talons were ready to fasten Krakto's wings to his back. His beak was poised to break his neck. Krakto watched him dive, faster and faster, closer and closer. And then, just as the eagle seemed certain to strike him, he hopped sideways and dived down the side of the ridge. The eagle was so heavy, his wings so short, that he was unable to manoeuvre. He landed heavily where Krakto had been, his wings flicking in frustration. Krakto soared past him. 'Strike one to me!' he taunted.

The great-eagle Moadeath tried again and again, diving at Krakto, swooping after him over the valleys, chasing him around the mountains. But Moadeath chasing Krakto was like a wet shag chasing a fresh damsel-fly.

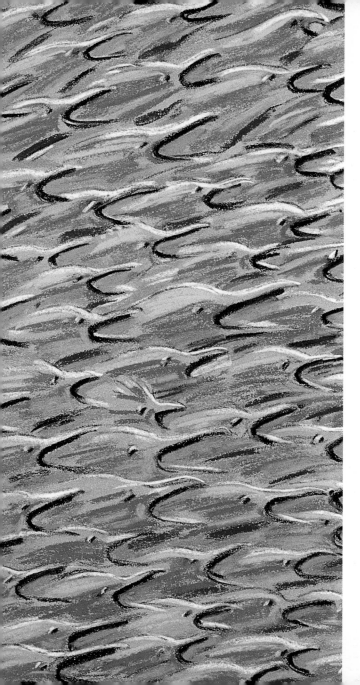

Krakto pranced along the ridges and tumbled through the air for four days and four nights. Slowly all the other birds of the world gathered to watch. 'Go, Krakto, go!' they screamed.

'Where were *you* when you were needed?' cried Krikta.

And then, when Ka bid the sun rise on the fifth day of the contest, Moadeath could be seen crouched behind a rock, his head slumped beneath his shoulders. Krakto was exhausted, too, but he had enough strength to raise his head and cry. 'D'you give up, d'you give up, d'you give up?'

And all the birds of the world cried, 'D'you give up, d'you give up, d'you give up?'

'Never!' raged Antika. 'Never! Get up, Moadeath! Get up!'

One more time, Moadeath pulled his wings together, lifted his head, and dived at Krakto. Closer he came, his claws jutting out, his beak ready for the kill. Again Krakto dived down the side of the ridge. But this time Moadeath followed him, diving faster and faster. Soon Krakto could smell Moadeath's stinking breath. He could almost feel the points of his talons tearing through his feathers. Krakto's strength was almost gone. With one last effort, he swerved sideways and flew into a cave.

Moadeath dived on. And on. And on. He had no strength left to open his wings. Every bird in the world flew over or perched on the mountains to watch.

Moadeath crashed into the foot of the mountain, so hard that he disappeared into the rock. 'Ouch!' cried Krikta as Moadeath's feathers scattered through the air. They plunged into the earth to grow again instantly as kamahi trees. These are all that remain today of the great-eagle Moadeath.

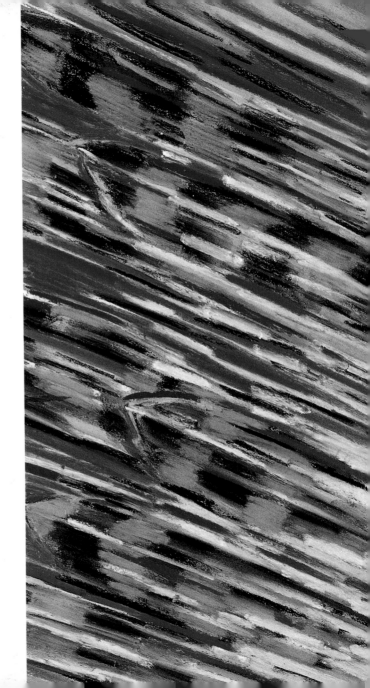

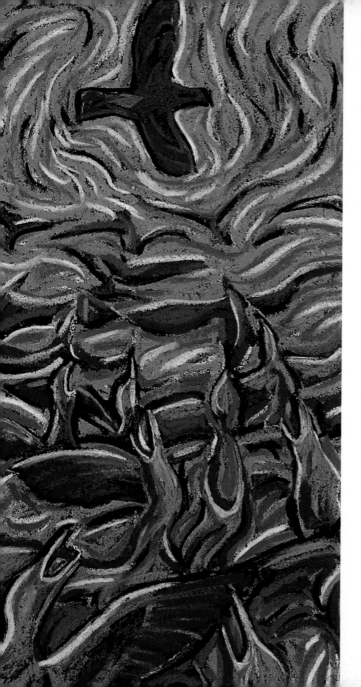

'One-nil to us !' cried Krikta. 'The winner is . . . the new Champion of the World is – representing on my right wing, Ka, the great bird of all birds – the one and only – Colossal Krakto!' Krakto flew a few circles to the applause of all the birds in the world.

Ka rose higher and higher above the mountains, spreading his wings so that a great shadow fell over Antika. 'Your champion has failed. Now you must never challenge again the natural order of things. Be gone! Return to the world's darkest corners!'

Antika did not want to go. He rose up to challenge Ka again. But now Ka was stronger. His eyes flashed bolts of lightning, striking Antika's head and wings. As flash after flash struck Antika, his eyes began to lose their fire, his head drooped and his wings shrivelled. Slowly he slid down and disappeared behind the mountains.

Krikta thought that he and Krakto should receive a reward for what they had done. As Ka folded his wings and began to drift away into the clouds of the morning sky, Krikta cried, 'So what about a better perch, Ka? What about a bigger share of the berries?'

Ka replied, 'Your reward is the return of the natural order of things. That is the reward for all birds. For I am part of you and you are part of me. Together we are the champions. Together we are all the world.'

As Ka disappeared into the clouds, Krikta heard another voice carried on the wind from the foot of the mountain. It was a voice as hard and cold as ice. 'For I am part of you, and you are part of me. Together we can change the world.'

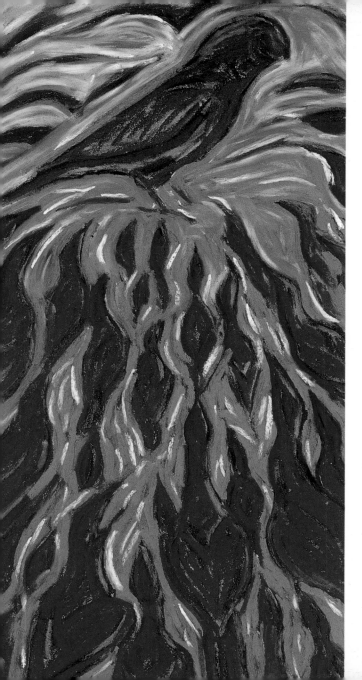

Before all the birds in the world flew back to their perches in the forest, along the rivers and by the great oceans, Krikta warned them, just as he warns us all even now. 'Remember that Antika did not agree to the rules. He will never agree to the rules. Watch for the bird who grows too greedy, watch for the plant that grows too fast, watch for the river that becomes too violent. Antika is not only in all of us but also in all things. If we do not remain on guard, he will rise again to challenge Ka and bring destruction to the world.'

PHILIP TEMPLE writes for children and adults. His adult novels include the enormously successful *Beak of the Moon* (1981) and its successor *Dark of the Moon* (1993). He has also written many works of non-fiction, including guides, books on mountaineering and early New Zealand exploration, photographic and political books. For his writing he has been awarded the Katherine Mansfield Fellowship in Menton and the Robert Burns Fellowship at the University of Otago.

CHRIS GASKIN is one of New Zealand's leading children's picture book and wildlife artists. His publications include *Joseph's Boat*; *Duckat*; *Picture Magic* (winner of the 1993 AIM Award for non-fiction); *A Walk to the Beach*; *Do Swans Surf?*; and *Remote the Land's Heart*. Chris is the first illustrator to have won the Russell Clark Award for illustration three times (1989, 1990, 1995).

Philip Temple and Chris Gaskin have worked together on a number of children's books, including *Moa, the story of a fabulous bird*; *The Legend of the Kea*; *The Story of the Kakapo*, which was an AIM Award winner in 1990; and *Kotuku, the flight of the white heron*, an AIM Honour Award winner in 1995.